David Prentice Menzies

Menzies Clan Society

David Prentice Menzies

Menzies Clan Society

ISBN/EAN: 9783743308084

Manufactured in Europe, USA, Canada, Australia, Japa

Cover: Foto ©ninafisch / pixelio.de

Manufactured and distributed by brebook publishing software
(www.brebook.com)

David Prentice Menzies

Menzies Clan Society

THE MENZIES

CLAN SOCIETY.

"SOIL NA MEINNRICH."

Toilleadh Dia a ni mise t.

ITS HISTORY, OBJECTS, BIOGRAPHIES, MEMBERS, &c.

BY

D. P. MENZIES, F.S.A., Scot.,

4 Holyrood Quadrant, or Weem Works, 34 Bishop Street, Glasgow.

LAIRD, MACINTYRE & CO., GLASGOW

THE NAME MENZIES.

The name Menzies is Celtic, and when Anglofied should be pronounced "Meingeis," the z being originally a Celtic "g," which is similar to the modern z with the tail. The Gaelic of the name is Meinnrigh, which signifies of a Majestic Countenance, or having a Royal-mien, or Regal-bearing.

BRANCH NAMES.

Mengies, Mennie, Means, Mein, Meine, Meyners, Minn, Minnus, Monzie, Dewar, MacMenzies, MacMinn, Mac-Monies:— See "What is My Tartan," by Frank Adam. p. 98.

HISTORY OF THE MENZIES CLAN SOCIETY

For several years prior to 1892 a strong desire was evinced among many gentlemen of the Clan Menzies, in various parts of the kingdom, that something should be done towards establishing a Menzies Clan Society. It was not, however, until the year 1892 that any active steps were taken. The first meeting, with this object in view, took place on the 17th May, 1892, being convened by D. P. Menzies, F.S.A., Scot., and held in the offices of Colonel James Menzies, of the Glasgow Highlanders, 68 Bath Street, Glasgow, where seven gentlemen of Clan Menzies met. These were—Colonel James Menzies, Walter Menzies, J.P. (then Parliamentary candidate for Central Glasgow), Lieutenant David Menzies of Balotnock, Rector Thomas Menzies, J.P., F.E.I.S., James Menzies and William Menzies, of the Phœnix Tube Works, Rutherglen, and D. P. Menzies, F.S.A., Scot., who was appointed hon. corresponding secretary. The result of the meeting was that "The Chief," Sir Robert Menzies, Bart., of Menzies, was communicated with, and at once gave his most hearty support to the movement, and a full Clan meeting called at Weem Hotel, Weem, on the 6th October, 1892, at 12 o'clock noon, presided over by "The Chief," when "THE MENZIES CLAN SOCIETY" was fully constituted. The Hereditary Chief, Junior Chief, Captain of Clan Menzies, and the Chieftains being acknowledged with the slogan or war cry of the Clan—*Geal is Dearg gu Brath*—Translated, "The Red and White for Ever" (given three times with cheers). The full details of both gatherings are given in the "Red and White" Book of Menzies, p. 447 to 450.

On the 24th February, 1893, the first Glasgow social gathering of Clan Menzies' was held in the Bath Hotel, when a large number of clansmen dined : Colonel James Menzies, Glasgow Highlanders, presiding. The croupiers being Lieutenant David Menzies of Balotnock, Colonel Duncan Menzies, Sutherland Highlanders, Rector Thomas Menzies, J.P., F.E.I.S., and D. P. Menzies, F.S.A., Scot., the hon. secretary, who intimated that in seven weeks over £200 had been subscribed to the funds of the Society.

The gathering was a most enthusiastic one, many of the Clan being in "The Kilt" of Menzies tartan, others wore Menzies tartan vests or neckties, and handkerchiefs of Menzies tartan. The toast of "The Chief" being given with Highland honours and the "War Cry" of the Clan.

Rector Thomas Menzies, in proposing the Clan Menzies Society Bursary Fund, said he hoped that clansmen who could, would give of their means to help to make up the £1000 to found the Bursary, and thereby put the Society in a position to help on the deserving of the Clan, to the higher professions of life.

The second annual business gathering was held at Weem Hotel, Weem on the 7th October, 1893. "The Chief," Sir Robert Menzies, Bart., of Menzies, presiding. There was a good turn out of clansmen from the surrounding Menzies country, and from Edinburgh, Falkirk, Stirling, Larbert, Coupar-Angus, Perth, Glasgow, &c. The Menzies hunting tartan, green and red, being displayed to great advantage in the Highland costumes—"The Kilt"—worn by "The Chief" and many of the Clan present. While the clansmen were assembling the Clan piper, Hamish Menzies, and the Chief's piper enlivened the scene by playing selections of stirring Highland tunes on their bagpipes. On the arrival of Sir Robert he was greeted by the slogan of the Clan and three cheers. Thereafter the business of the Society was proceeded with, the hereditary members being acknowledged, and the office-bearers being elected for the year. The secretary intimated that the total funds then stood about £302 7s. 6d. On the conclusion of the business "The Chief" and clansmen sat down to lunch, when a very pleasant and social time was spent.

On the 31st January, 1894, the second Glasgow social gathering was held in the Bath Hotel, Walter Menzies, J.P., in the chair. The croupiers being Lieutenant David Menzies of Edinmuck, Rector Thomas Menzies, J.P., F.E.I.S., and the secretary. The dinner consisted of Scotch Kail, Scotch Haggis, &c., and the feature of the evening was a Highland reel danced by four Menzies', in Highland costume—"The Kilt"—the Menzies hunting tartan. During the evening, songs, speeches, music, &c., were given, and much appreciated.

The third annual gathering of the Society was held at Weem on the 25th September, 1894, where "The Chief," Sir Robert Menzies, Bart., of Menzies, had received his jubilee, being 50 years Chief of Clan Menzies, and inheritor of the ancient baronial estates of Menzies on the 16th August, 1894. The Clan, to commemorate which, raised a sum of money, and at the request of The Chief, this was sunk in the Society to form a "The Sir Robert Menzies Jubilee Benevolent Fund," and founded on the 77th birthday of Sir Robert, 25th September, 1894. At the meeting, the Chief was received with the slogan of the Clan and three cheers, with the best wishes of his Clan for long life. The Clan acknowledging him as Hereditary Chief, and also the other hereditary members of the Clan, and elected the office-bearers for the year. In the great Jubilee gathering afterwards, the Clan presented Sir Robert with a large illuminated address

in a carved and gilded frame. Full particulars of the whole proceedings are given in the "Red and White" Book of Menzies, pages 463 to 474.

On the 22nd March, 1895, the third annual social gathering in Glasgow of the Clan, was held in the Bath Hotel, where there was a large turnout. The full dress Menzies tartan, red and white, and the Menzies hunting tartan, green and red, being displayed to great advantage in "The Kilt." Plaids, and hose of the Highland dress worn by many of the clansmen, and also in the costumes of the ladies. The hall was decorated with the portraits of the Chiefs of Clan Menzies, from Junior Chief Captain Robert Menzies, who fought at the battle of Killiecrankie, along with his brother Captain James Menzies of Comrie, under General McKay; also the portraits of Chief Sir Alexander, 2nd Bart., Chief Sir Robert Menzies, 3rd Bart., who entertained Bonnie Prince Charlie for several days before the battle of Culloden at Castle Menzies, for which he nearly lost his head; Chief Sir Ian Menzies, 4th Bart., Chief Sir Robert, 5th Bart., Chief Sir Neil, 6th Bart., who raised a guard of honour of 200 Clansmen for the Queen and Prince Albert, on their first visit to the Highlands in 1842. This guard were all dressed in the red and white Menzies tartan; and the portrait of the present Chief Sir Robert Menzies, 7th Bart.; also the present Junior Chief Captain Neil James Menzies, and Fletcher N. Menzies, the Captain of Clan Menzies. A short description of each portrait being given by the secretary.

The gathering was opened by a reception by Walter Menzies, Esq., J.P., and Colonel James Menzies, of the Glasgow Highlanders. The party, on leaving the drawing-room for the dancing hall, were headed by the pipers playing the Menzies Bannockburn bagpipes to the national tune of "Scots wha hae wi' Wallace bled."

The programme, consisting of dances, songs, &c., which was enthusiastically entered into and kept up till 2 a.m.

A source of great interest to the company was the ancient "Menzies Bannockburn Bagpipes," which led the Clan into action at that great battle. The only parts of the original left are the chanter, the blowpipe, and half the drones, the bag and sockets being restorations. Yet, notwithstanding their worm-eaten condition, they were refitted, so as to cause them to play as well as the modern pipe, but not so loud, as they have only one drone, but the air or melody is heard more distinctly.

The fourth annual business gathering was held at Weem on the 31st August, 1894, and was presided over by "The Chief," Sir Robert Menzies, Bart.; there was a good attendance of members from Forfar, Stirling, Blairgowrie, Coupar-Angus, Falkirk, Dublin, Glasgow, &c., and districts. Many wearing the "Garb of Old Gaul"—The Kilt—in which the Menzies tartan was shown to advantage. After the usual annual business was

transacted, the clansmen acknowledged (with the other hereditary members) Robert Murray Menzies, hereditary chieftain of the Menzies', of Bolfracks, he being the eldest surviving son of Captain Gilbert Menzies, and grandson of Major Archibald Menzies, both of the "Black Watch," the 42nd Highlanders, and who were both retoured heirs of the ancient Menzies Barony of Bolfracks.

On the conclusion of the above business the company adjourned into the dining-room, where, presided over by the Chief, they dined, where there was much pleasant interchange of Clan sentiment and friendly feeling.

On the evening of Thursday, 28th November, 1895, the fourth annual social Glasgow gathering was held in the Bath Hotel, when there was a large and brilliant turnout of ladies and gentlemen of the Clan. Almost every gentleman of Clan Menzies was attired in Highland costume—"The Kilt"; everywhere was to be seen the Menzies tartans, crests, badges, and other emblems of the Clan, the "Red and White" tartan of the Clan being easily distinguished by its bright artistic colour, but the hunting tartan, green and red, predominated. The dancing-hall was gaily decorated with large armourial shields of "The Chief" and chieftains of the various branches of the Clan, viz. :—"The Chief" Menzies of Menzies, 1037, red and white, Perthshire; The Menzies' of Enoch and Durrisdeer, 1370 (black and white); The Menzies' of Rotmell, Perthshire, 1510; The Menzies' of Pitfodels, Aberdeenshire, 1672, red and ermine; The Menzies' of Aberdeen, 1672; The Menzies' of Culdares, Perthshire, 1672; The ancient arms of the Menzies' of Bolfracks, Perthshire; The Menzies' of Shian and Glenquich, Perthshire, 1672; The Menzies' of Gledstanes and Edinburgh, 1672. Each of the escutcheons were different in shape, their outlines being taken from ancient sculptures and other authorities of the Clan. There was exhibited to the company "The Menzies Bannockburn Claymore," or two-handed sword, wielded at that great battle by the Chief of the Clan, Sir Alexander Menzies, a fellow patriot with Sir William Wallace, and King Robert the Bruce against the English for the freedom and liberty of Scotland. The sword is somewhat similar to the "Wallace Sword," but is about 7 inches longer, being 58 inches long, and weighs about 7 lbs. The Clan had also another relic of their ancestors submitted for their inspection, viz. :—"The Queen Mary Menzies Bronze Cannon," dated 1553, which bears the cypher of the Earl of Arran, then Regent of Scotland, "I. H.," and the escutcheon of the Hamiltons. These were lent by the Chief, Sir Robert Menzies, Baronet of Menzies, and submitted by D. P. Menzies, F.S.A., Scot., and were of great interest to the company. Altogether, the scene was brilliant and animated. The proceedings commenced with a reception, the guests being received by David Menzies of Babornock in full Highland costume, and Rector Thomas Menzies, J.P.,

F.E.I.S., in the absence of Walter Menzies, J.P., and Colonel James
Menzies, of the Glasgow Highlanders, the guests being introduced by the
Hon. Secretary, after which the company proceeded to the large hall
headed by James Menzies, the Clan Piper from Castle Menzies, where the
dancing was commenced by a Highland Reel, and with great spirit kept
up to an early hour next morning. During the evening Highland and
other songs were rendered in magnificent style and exquisite taste by Ian
Menzies (Kenmore), with others of the Clan. Hamish Menzies, the Clan
Piper, danced the Highland fling and the sword dance with grace and
agility, and several others of the Clan and friends lent to the music of the
gathering. At the close the company joined hands and sang "Auld Lang
Syne," and gave three cheers with the slogan of the Clan, "Geal's Dearg
gu Bràth"—"The Red and White for Ever."

The funds of the Society are in a flourishing condition, as will be seen
from the undernoted details :—

			£	s	d
Total Amount of Bursary Fund, 7th September, 1896.			362	0	8
,,	,,	of Chief's Benevolent Fund, ...	50	5	3
,,	,,	in hands of Treasurer, ...	26	16	8
,,	,,	in hands of Secretary, ...	12	0	3
			£451	2	10

OFFICE BEARERS.

Hereditary Chief.

Sir ROBERT MENZIES, Baronet of Menzies: Seats—Castle Menzies,
Rannoch Lodge, Foss House, and Farleyer, Perthshire.

Hereditary Junior Chief.

Captain NEIL JAMES MENZIES, of Menzies, late of Scots Guards, Castle
Menzies, Aberfeldy, Perthshire, and Guards' Club, London.

Hereditary Captain of the Clan.

Captain FLETCHER NORTON MENZIES, Esq., of Menzies, Balnakill,
Ballinluig, Perthshire.

Hereditary Chieftains of Septs.

ROBERT MURRAY MENZIES, Esq., of Bolfracks, "Baron Bolfracks,"
Wester Livlands, Stirling.

Lieut. W. GEORGE S. STUART MENZIES, Esq., of Culdares, Aikenway,
Craig Ellachie, N.B.

Major W. J. B. STEWART MENZIES, Esq., of Chesthill, Gordon Highlanders,
Chesthill, Glenlyon, Perthshire.

Hon. Corresponding Secretary.

D. P. MENZIES, Esq., F.S.A., Scot., Holyrood Quadrant, and
Weem Works, 59 Bishop Street, Glasgow.

President.

W. D. GRAHAM MENZIES, Esq., J.P., of Hallyburton and Pitcur,
Coupar-Angus, N.B., and 6 Hereford Gardens, London, W.C.

9

Convener.

WALTER MENZIES, Esq., J.P., East Park, and Phœnix Works, Rutherglen.

Vice-Presidents.

Colonel JAMES MENZIES, V.D., Glasgow Highlanders, Mount Fergin,
Bothwell, and 65 Bath Street, Glasgow.

Colonel DUNCAN MENZIES, J.P., 1st Sutherland Highlanders, R.V.,
Biarich, Rogart, Sutherlandshire, and Westwood, Inverness.

Colonel ROBERT MENZIES, Q.R.V.B.R.S., V.D., J.P., of Viewfield,
46 Drummond Place, Edinburgh.

ROBERT MENZIES, Esq., J.P., Tirinie, Weem, Aberfeldy, Perthshire.

Major ARCHIBALD MENZIES, Queen's R.V. Brigade, 3 St. David
Street, Edinburgh.

Dr. JAMES IRVINE MENZIES, 47 Earl's Court Square, S. Kensington, London.

Captain DUNCAN MENZIES, C.E., Queen's R.V.B. Highland Companies,
37 York Place, Edinburgh.

Hon. District Secretaries.

ARCHIBALD MENZIES, Esq., S.S.C., 3 St. David Street, Edinburgh.
(For Edinburgh District.)

JAMES STEWART MENZIES, Esq., 9 Rosewood Terrace, and Dundee, Perth,
and London Shipping Company, Dundee.
(For Perth, Dundee, and District.)

Hon. Treasurer for Bursary Fund.

Rector THOMAS MENZIES, J.P., F.E.I.S., Hutcheson's Schools,
Crown Street, Glasgow.

Hon. General Treasurer.

ROBERT MENZIES, Esq., Proprietor, Weem Hotel, Aberfeldy.
(And Secretary for Weem, Aberfeldy, and District.)

10

Council.

Lieutenant DAVID MENZIES, Esq., of Balornock, late Glasgow Highlanders.
7 Buckingham Terrace, Glasgow.
JOHN LOW MENZIES, Esq., 100 Eglinton Street, Glasgow. *(Auditor.)*
JAMES MENZIES, Esq., 30 Royal Crescent, Edinburgh.
ROBERT MENZIES, Esq., 129 Main Street, Maryhill, Glasgow.
THOMAS MENZIES, Esq., Shipbuilder and Engineer, 8 Hermitage Place,
Leith.
Dr. DOUGLAS C. MENZIES, Rosebery House, Inverkeithing.
JAMES MENZIES, Esq., Coach Proprietor, Aberfeldy.
ADAM MENZIES, Esq., Ironmonger, Pitlochry.
JAMES MENZIES, Esq., Beechwood, Rutherglen, Glasgow. *(Auditor.)*
WILLIAM MENZIES, Esq., Fernbank, Rutherglen, Glasgow.
JOHN MENZIES (Parish Councillor), Burnside Terrace, Camelon, Falkirk.
ROBERT MENZIES, Esq., Bow Street, and 24 Queen Street, Stirling
CHARLES RAMAGE MENZIES, Esq., 87 Cambridge Street, Glasgow.
PETER MENZIES, 7 Janefield Place, Maryhill; or, 33 Gordon St., Glasgow.
JOHN MENZIES, Esq., Leaf Merchant, Aberfeldy.
WILLIAM MENZIES, Esq., 171 Crookston Street, S.S., Glasgow.

Piper to the Menzies Clan Society.

Mr. JAMES MENZIES, Shenvail, Weem, Aberfeldy.

Note.—As the Society pay an annual license for the use of the armorial
bearings, every member is entitled to wear or use the Arms or Crest,
as given by the Excise, viz. :—

"By any Officer or Member of a Club, or Society, using at the Club, or on the
business of the Society, any Armorial Bearings for the use of which such Club, or
Society, have taken out a Licence."

The Menzies Clan Society.

OBJECTS.

The objects of "THE MENZIES CLAN SOCIETY" shall be (1) To cultivate and strengthen the true Celtic ties of Family, the spirit of Kin and Clanship, the promotion of friendly and social intercourse between the Members of the Clan. (2) The higher education of young men of the name of Menzies, and to provide specially, a free, or assisted, secondary education, to qualify them to compete for 'The James Menzies Bursary," thereby giving them the means of a University Curriculum for "The Arts," and if this existing Bursary should prove insufficient, to collect funds to provide such other Bursaries as may be found necessary. (3) To render assistance to any of the name, in such circumstances as may require aid. (4) The collecting and preserving of History, Traditions, Poetry, Music, Antiquities of the Arts and Sculpture, and Relics of persons or events connected with The Clan Menzies, and to form a collection of such, to be placed in the hands of Sir Robert Menzies, as Custodian, in a room at Castle Menzies, for reference and exhibition. (5) The wearing of the Menzies Tartan and the Highland Dress, for which the Clan has always been noted. (6) To found Prizes for competition, to encourage the cultivation of Literary Composition, Poetry, Music, ease and eloquence in Public Speaking, and excellence in Art, &c., &c.

CONSTITUTION.

(1) The Society shall be called "THE MENZIES CLAN SOCIETY" (Siol na Meinnrich).

(2) The Society shall be non-sectarian and non-political.

MEMBERS.

(3) The Members shall consist of Gentlemen of the surname of Menzies. Ladies of the name by birth being also eligible for membership, and *sept* names who have branched off from the Clan, and shall be elected by the vote or ballot of the directorate of the district in which they join, after having been proposed and seconded. The sons and daughters of Members, under 18 years of age, may be enrolled as Junior Members, Associate or Honorary.

ASSOCIATE MEMBERS.

(4) Associate Members shall consist of Gentlemen, whose mothers, wives, or grand-parents are of the name of Menzies: they, however, shall not have any say in the affairs of the Society, but will have the privilege of recommending applicants.

HONORARY MEMBERS.

(5) Honorary Members shall consist of Ladies and Gentlemen, who are in any way connected, friendly, or interested in the Clan, or who make donations, or otherwise be serviceable to the Clan and Society, but shall have no say in its affairs.

SUBSCRIPTIONS.

(6) The Annual Subscription of Members, Associate Members, and Honorary Members, shall be 10s annually, payable on or before the 1st January each year, with the exception of such as are resident in the rural parts of the Highlands, or serving in H.M.S. as non-commissioned Officers,

or in humble circumstances: in such cases the Subscriptions shall be 2 6 for any sum between 10 - and 2 6 per annum, and any person being admitted as a Member, may become a Life Member on payment of not less than £10 10 -: Ladies, 45 5/-. A Bursary will be founded out of the Life Member Subscriptions to be called "The Menzies Clan Society Bursary," for which it is sought to raise £1000. Members whose Subscriptions may be in arrears shall not be entitled to vote, or have any say in the business of the Society until paid. The Subscriptions of Juniors shall be half that of Adult Members.

That no Member can be eligible for any office unless his Subscription has been paid up to date.

That any Member wishing to become a Life Member, who has already been paying into the funds as an ordinary Member, may compound within three years, and have the amount paid in that time deducted from the £10 10 - Life Member Subscription.

OFFICE-BEARERS. MEETINGS, &C.

(7) The business of the Clan shall be managed by a Council, consisting of the Hereditary Chief, Sir Robert Menzies, Bart., of that Ilk, Hereditary Chieftains, Captains, &c. As the Clan was constituted of old, with a President, three or seven Vice-Presidents, Convener, two Secretaries, Treasurer, and seven to twenty-one of a Council. One-third of the Council retire each year, but all Office-Bearers (except Hereditary) shall be eligible for re-election annually. The Annual General Meeting of the Council and Members to be intimated, and the next place of Meeting to be arranged at each Meeting. Each City or District may, if strong enough, have its own Office-Bearers, consisting of President, Vice-President, Secretary, Treasurer, and Committee, but only at the Annual General Meeting of the Clan and Council, can any alterations be made in the Constitution, Laws, &c., of the Clan, and three months' notice of any such proposed alteration must be lodged in writing, and

in detail, with the Secretary. The Clan at these Meetings may elect qualified Members as Bards or Pipers to the Clan. Seven to three Members to be a quorum, and not less than one-third of the Members on any occasion of alterations of the Constitution, Laws, &c. Each District may arrange Lectures, Meetings, &c., in prosecution of the objects of the Society. For the Meetings of Council or District Committees, three shall form a quorum.

FUNDS. AUDITORS. BANK ACCOUNT. &C.

(8) The Treasurer shall receive and disburse all moneys due to or by the Society. He shall keep exact accounts of his intromissions, and his books shall be patent at all times to the Members of Council; he shall prepare and submit to the Annual Meeting of the Society, a yearly statement of his intromissions, which shall be audited by two Members to be appointed by the Council. The Funds of the Society shall be lodged in a bank in the name of "THE MENZIES CLAN SOCIETY," and the Bank Account shall be operated upon by Cheques drawn by the Treasurer, and countersigned by the Secretary and one of the Vice-Presidents.

INVESTMENTS AND PROPERTY.

(9) The Property or Funds of the Society requiring to be invested, may be invested in any investment competent to gratuitous Trustees, by Statute or at Common Law, and shall be held in the name of Three Trustees to be appointed by the Council, and no investment shall be made or varied except by the direction of the Council.

DONATIONS, LEGACIES. GIFTS. &C.

(10) Donations and Legacies may be left for the purposes of the Society generally, or may bear the Donor's names, if for any special purpose or object, for the benefit of the Clan Menzies, these may be made payable to the Hereditary Chief, or to the President, Secretary, or Treasurer for the time being.

as Trustees for "THE MENZIES CLAN SOCIETY." Gifts also of Antiquities, Manuscripts, Arms, Armour, Works of Art, Sculpture, Musical Instruments, Books or Music to or by any of the name of Menzies, or relics of any description connected with the Clan or its history. These may be made over to the Society in the same way, such to be placed in the hands of the Hereditary Chief, Sir Robert Menzies, Bart., of that Ilk, as custodian, and placed along with such as may be acquired by purchase, or otherwise, at Castle Menzies.

GRANTS FOR EDUCATION AND BURSARY.

(11) Higher Education. Applicants of the name wishing to pursue their studies at Secondary Schools, to prepare and qualify them to compete for "The Menzies Bursaries," they must submit the course of study and their specific object, or the profession they propose to follow, and the progress made (in the event of the applicant having been at school), must be certified by the Teacher or Teachers. The applicant must be recommended to the notice of the Society by a Member or Associate Member, and if required, undergo an examination, at such time and place as shall be most convenient for all parties, to the satisfaction of the Council, when the Council may allow a sum towards this object, varying, according to circumstances, from £5 per annum.

BYE-LAWS AND SUB-COMMITTEES.

(12) The Council of the Menzies Clan shall from time to time make such Bye-Laws or Regulations as they may consider necessary, with power to them to alter or vary such should they see fit; and the Council may appoint any Sub-Committee or Sub-Committees they may consider requisite for carrying out the purposes of the Society. Such Sub-Committee or Sub-Committees may be formed from among themselves or in conjunction with such Members of the Society as they shall deem expedient.

The "James Menzies" Bursary.

FOUNDED 1837.

£50 per Year : Open to all of the Name of Menzies.

"The 'Menzies Bursaries (Arts).' The late James Menzies, Esq., Glasgow, by his will, dated 3rd November, 1837, left a sum of money to establish four Bursaries at either of the Universities : Edinburgh, Glasgow or St. Andrews, tenable for four years, one to be given each year. The value of each Bursary is £50 per annum, but varies at the discretion of the Patrons. The Patrons are "The Chief," Menzies of Menzies, and the Parish Ministers of Dull, Weem, and Forting...l. In the first place, the kindred of the Testator; secondly, persons of the name of Menzies; thirdly, those born on the Menzies Estates will be preferred, provided always that they shall be found properly qualified by previous examination; and failing these, the Patrons can present such as shall be found best qualified after due examination :—English Reading and Writing & Dictation; Arithmetic, as far as Decimal Fractions; English text books ; Latin *Cæsar de Bello Gallico*, first four books; and to translate a piece of English into Latin : Greek, *Xenophon's Anabasis*, first three books. Bursars to attend, in one of the above Universities, the Classes in their regular order for the M.A. Degree. Candidates are requested to send their names to the Factor of the Menzies Estates for the time being, Camserney Cottage, near Aberfeldy, on or before 14th September. *From Glasgow University Calendar.*

———◆•◆•◆———

The Sir Robert Menzies Benevolent Fund.

This Fund was founded to commemorate the Jubilee of The Chief, Sir Robert Menzies, Baronet—"Nan Meinnrich"—by the Clan, on the 2... September, 1894, for the purpose of relieving the wants of those of the name in distress. All subscriptions to it go to the Capital Sum, the interest of which is to be used for benevolent purposes. This Fund is always ready to receive subscriptions of any sum annually, or at any time. Clansmen are urgently requested to subscribe to this good object annually, whatever sum, however small. Amount of Capital Fund, 14th July, 1896, £56 3s. 5d.

The Menzies Clan Society Bursary.

FOUNDED 1892

TRUSTEES.

Colonel JAMES MENZIES, 68 Bath Street, Glasgow, Mount Fergan, Bothwell.

WALTER MENZIES, Esq., J.P., Phoenix Tube Works, Rutherglen.

Major ARCHIBALD MENZIES, S.S.C., 3 St. David Street, Edinburgh.

Rector THOMAS MENZIES, J.P., F.E.I.S., Hon. Treasurer, Hutchens us Grammar School, Crown Street, Glasgow, to whom applicants may apply.

OBJECTS.

The Objects are to take up what is not adequately provided for in "The James Menzies Bursary," viz.:—To assist Clansmen through the Universities as Medical Doctors, Civil Engineers, Chemists, or other University Classes necessary to fit them for special scientific professions, and also to assist those in H.M.S. as non-commissioned officers or privates through classes, &c., necessary to procure their commissions, or civil service positions.

In the event of there being no applicants under the above Objects, the annual income of the Fund may be applied to benevolent purposes, or the purchase of Clan relics, or the erection of memorials to distinguished Clansmen, or of events in the History of the Clan, &c.

At the first meeting of the Menzies Clan Society Council, in the rooms of Colonel Robert Menzies, 17th November, 1892, it was proposed by the Hon. Secretary, and seconded by Colonel James Menzies, and unanimously carried, to raise £1000 by life member subscriptions and otherwise, this sum becoming the sunk and invested fund of the Bursary, the interest only from which should be applied for the objects herein stated, the fund kept entirely in the hands of the MENZIES CLAN Society and the Trustees appointed by it. The whole funds are the private property of the Society, and are not in any way controlled or connected with the Universities or Government Education Scheme, the Society and its Trustees only, having power to deal with the Bursary Funds and dispose of the revenue. The Trustees may put their schemes in operation on its funds reaching £500.

*Roll of Life Members of the Menzies Clan Society who
have subscribed not less than £10 10., or Ladies.
£3 3., and which sums form part of the Bursary
Fund of the principal sum of £1000. to be raised to
Found the Menzies Clan Society Bursary.*

Sir Robert Menzies, Bart., of that Ilk : Seats—Castle Menzies,
    Rannoch Lodge, Foss House, and Farleyer, Weem, by
    Aberfeldy, ... £10 10 0
Captain Neil James Menzies, of Menzies, late Scots Guards,
    Castle Menzies, near Aberfeldy, and Guards' Club,
    London, - 10 10 0
Major Archibald Menzies, S.S.C., 12 Mentone Terrace, and 3
    St. David Street, Edinburgh, ... 10 10 0
Lieut. David Menzies, of Balornock, 7 Buckingham Terrace,
    Glasgow, ... 10 10 0
D. P. Menzies, F.S.A., Scot., 4 Holyrood Quadrant, and 30
    Bishop Street, Glasgow, ... 10 10 0
F. C. Graham Menzies, Esq., of Hallyburton, Coupar-Angus. 10 10 0
Colonel Duncan Menzies, J.P., Blarich, Rogart, Sutherland-
    shire, and Westwood, Inverness. 10 10 0
Captain Duncan Menzies, C.E., 30 York Place, Edinburgh, - 10 10 0
Colonel James Menzies, Mount Fergan, Bothwell, and 68 Bath
    Street, Glasgow, ... 10 10 0
Dr. James Irvine Menzies, 47 Earl's Court Square, South
    Kensington, London. 10 10 0
James Menzies, Esq., Beechwood, Rutherglen, Glasgow, - 10 10 0
John Graham Menzies, Esq., of Esewick Park, York, and
    Hallyburton, - 10 10 0
John Menzies, Esq., Lead Merchant, Aberfeldy. . . - 10 10 0
James Menzies, Esq., Chemist, 30 Royal Terrace, Edinburgh, 10 10 0
Surgeon John Duncan Menzies, Royal Navy, H.M.S. Sanspariel,
    Mediterranean, died 12th November, 1895, . . 10 10 0
John Low Menzies, Esq., 98 Eglinton Street, S.S., Glasgow, - 10 10 0
Robert Murray Menzies, Esq., " Baron Bolfracks of Bolfracks,"
    Wester Livilands, Stirling, ... 10 10 0
Colonel Robert Menzies, J.P., V.D., Q.R.V.B.R.S., of View-
    field, Harthill, Lanarkshire, and 40 Drummond Place,
    Edinburgh, ... 10 10 0
Robert Menzies, Esq., Bow Street, and 24 George Street,
    Stirling, - 10 16 0

Robert A. M. Menzies, Esq., Hawkfield House, Restalrig Road,
    Leith : or, The Burgh Cabinet Works Company, 172
    Easter Road, Edinburgh, ... 10 10 6
Robert Menzies, Esq., J.P., Tirinie, near Weem, by Aberfeldy, £10 10 0
Robert Menzies, Esq., 7 Innerfield Place, Maryhill, Glasgow, - 10 10 6
Rector Thomas Menzies, J.P., F.E.I.S., of Hutcheson's Schools,
    Crown Street, Glasgow, ... 10 10 0
Walter Menzies, Esq., J.P., East Park, Rutherglen, and
    Phœnix Works, Glasgow, ... 10 10 0
William Menzies, Esq., Fern Bank, Rutherglen, Glasgow, - 10 10 6
William D. Graham Menzies, Esq., J.P., of Hallyburton and
    Piteur, Cupar-Angus, and of 6 Hereford Gardens, Hyde
    Park, London, ... 10 10 0
Lieut. Wm. George Stuart Menzies, of Culdares, Aikenway,
    Craig Ellachie, N.B., ... 10 10 0
Major Wm. J. B. Stewart Menzies, of Chesthill, Glenlyon, by
    Aberfeldy, ... 10 10 0
William J. Menzies, Esq., of Stretton Hall, Malpas, Cheshire, 10 10 0

Lady Life Members.

Miss Egidia Charlotte Menzies, of Menzies, Castle Menzies,
    near Aberfeldy, Perthshire, ... £3 3 0
Miss Jessie C. Menzies, 4 Holyrood Quadrant, W., Glasgow, - 3 3 0
Mrs. Menzies, Dublin Street, Edinburgh, died 27th Oct., 1894. 3 3 0

Miss Ella Menzies, Mrs. Fraser now, Westwood, Inverness, - 3 3 0
Ann Menzies, Mrs. MacNab, Fife Arms Hotel, Braemar, . 3 3 0
Miss Pauline Menzies, Churchill House, Ventnor, Isle of Wight. 3 3 0
Mrs. Robert E. H. Norton, née Menzies, Coombe Croft,
    Norbiton, Surrey, ... 3 3 0

From the Annual Glasgow Gathering Surplus, Session 1893, - £1 0 0
From the Annual Glasgow Gathering and Dance Surplus,
    Session 1894, ... 4 5 0
From the Ordinary Funds, through Hon. Secy., Session 1894, 15 0 0
From the Annual Glasgow Gathering and Dance Surplus,
    Session 1895, ... 3 10 0
From the Ordinary Funds, through Hon. Secy., Session 1895, 12 17 0

Ordinary Members subscribing 10/- per annum, to the Funds of the Menzies Clan Society.

A. J. P. Menzies, M.A., Advocate, 6 Great King Street, Edinburgh.
Adam Menzies, Lead Merchant, Pitlochry.
Barrister Alfred Irvine Menzies, M.A. Oxon., 47 Earl's Court Square, W., London.
Captain Fletcher Norton Menzies, of Menzies, Balmacneil, Ballinluig.
Charles Menzies, 27 Cluny Drive, Edinburgh.
Daniel Menzies, 28 Ardgowan Street, Greenock, W.; for, 28 Waterloo Street, Glasgow.
Dr. David Menzies, M.B., F.R.C.S., 20 Rutland Square, Edinburgh.
Dr. Douglas C. Menzies, Roseberry House, Inverkeithing.
Dr. Duncan M. Menzies, M.A., M.B., 4 Harewood Square, N.W., London.
Dr. Henry Menzies, B.A. Camb., 47 Earl's Court Square, W., London.
Dr. James Menzies, Park Villa, Gabyshiels.
Dr. James Herbert Menzies, M.R.C.S., 47 Earl's Court Square, London.
Dr. William T. Menzies, B.Sc., M.R.C.P., Rainhill County Asylum, Lancashire.
Duncan Murray Menzies, Bolfracks, The Knoll, Dipton, New Zealand.
George Menzies, Factor to the Duke of Sutherland, Trentham, Stoke-on-Trent.
James Menzies, Post Master, Aberfeldy.
James Menzies, Agent, 60 Shamrock Street, Glasgow.
James Stewart Menzies (Bolfracks), 9 Rosewood Terrace, Dundee.
John Menzies, Farmer, Croftcunnick, near Aberfeldy.
John Menzies, J.P., C.E., Mendbark, Carnarvon, Wales.
John Menzies, 9 Rosburn Terrace, Edinburgh.
John Henry Menzies, Esq., J.P., of Menzies Bay, Menzies Bay, Canterbury, New Zealand.
John Herbert Menzies, Trentham, Stoke-on-Trent.
Lieut. George Fielding Menzies, 1st Battalion South Lancashire Regiment, Athlone.
Middy Leslie Menzies, Royal Navy, of H.M.S. Blake.
Colonel Oswald Menzies, Inspector General Home Department, Punjab, India, 32 North Park Road, Ealing.
Professor Allan Menzies, B.A., etc., St. Andrews University, St. Andrews.
R. T. Menzies, Esq., o Gordon, Woodralls, Co., Madras, India.
Rev. Canon Frederick Menzies, of Brasenose College, Oxford, Shedford Lodge, Madeira Road, Bournemouth.
Robert Menzies, Proprietor, Weem Hotel, Weem, near Aberfeldy.
Robert Menzies, Estate Office, Haverland, Norwich.

Robert Hewitt Menzies, San Raface Marin, California, San Francisco, U.S., America.
Samuel Menzies, 1 Dowanvale Terrace, Glasgow.
Thomas James Menzies, M.A., B.Sc., *Hutchesons' Grammar Schools*, Crown Street, Glasgow.
Thomas Menzies, Ship Builder and Engineer, Leith.
Thomas Menzies, 23 Merchiston Road, Edinburgh.
Ex-Bailie Thomas Menzies, 1 Abercromby Place and King Street, Stirling.
Thomas Graham Menzies, C.E., Camden Place, Stirling.
William Menzies, Tea Merchant, 171 Crookston Street, S.S., Glasgow.
William Menzies, C.E., 1 Grosvenor Villas, and 56 Side, Newcastle-on-Tyne.
William J. Menzies, W.S., Camera House, Grange Loan, Edinburgh.
William John Menzies, of Balornock, The Grammerics, Bournemouth-East.
William Paterson Menzies, Accountant, 113 West Regent St., Glasgow.
William R. Murray Menzies, Esq., Bedruacks, Ardeer, Norwood, Ceylon, India.
Miss Elizabeth Menzies, 63 Great King Street, Edinburgh.
Miss Isabella Menzies, Home Lodge, Viewforth, Edinburgh.
Miss S. Jahana Menzies-Shaw, West Brookfield, Mass., U.S. America.
Flora Menzies (Mrs. Bruce), 125 North John Street, Glasgow.
Mrs. Susan Ann Menzies Shaw, Joined at the age of 82, 11/10/95, West Brookfield, Mass., U.S. America.

Associate and Honorary Members subscribing 10 - annually.

Alfred Menzies Jones, Esq., of Ravenswood, Nerblton, Surrey.
Archibald Gray Bruce, 125 North John Street, Glasgow.
Lieutenant A. Robertson Stark, 3rd Battalion Black Watch, Royal Highlanders, Ticehurst, Sussex.
Rev. Charles Menzies, Lambrick, M.A., Grandson of the late General Sir Charles Menzies, Tideswell, Buxton, Derbyshire.
Rev. George Menzies, Lambrick, Grandson of the late General Sir Charles Menzies, 8 Sidney Square, Stepney, London.

Members subscribing 5 - per annum to the Funds of the Menzies Clan Society.

A. Graham Menzies, 5 Kelvinside Terrace, West, Glasgow.
Alexander Menzies, Proprietor, Railway Hotel, Coupar, Angus.
Alexander Menzie, Insurance Secretary, 107 Wellington Street, Glasgow.
Alexander Menzies, 723 New City Road, Glasgow.
Alexander Duff Menzies, 22 Lansdowne Crescent, Glasgow.

Alexander Menzies, Forester to the Duke of Queensberry, Carrantoot, Thornhill.

Alfred Ernest Menzies, 22 Haldwood Road, Liverpool.

Arthur William Menzies, Menaibank, Carnarvon, Wales.

Charles Ramage Menzies, Carver and Gilder, 87 Cambridge St., Glasgow.

Colin Menzies, Jun., Architect, 2 West Regent Street, Glasgow.

Duncan Menzies, Houston Street, S.S., Glasgow.

Fredric Norton Menzies, Menaibank, Carnarvon, Wales.

George Menzies, Glencairn Cottage, Saltcoats.

George Mennie, Publisher, 57 West Nile Street, Glasgow.

Henry Fisher Menzies, 35 Warrender Park Road, Edinburgh.

H. S. Menzies, c o Mrs. Duncan, 42 Marchmont Road, Edinburgh.

James Menzies, Medical Student, 18 Waverley Gardens, Crossmyloof, Glasgow.

James Menzies, Lytchett Minster, Poole.

James Sinclair Menzies, 66 Shamrock Street, Glasgow.

Robert E. Menzies, Virden, Manitoba, Canada, West.

Robert Menzies, c o Mrs. Gillan, 66 Shamrock Street, Glasgow.

Sergeant John Menzies, 92nd Gordon Highlanders, Aldershot.

James Clerk Menzies, The Portland, Portland Oregon, U.S. America.

John Menzies, c o Sir Donald Currie, 40 St. Enoch Square, Glasgow.

John Menzies (Parish Councillor), Burnside Terrace, Camelon, Falkirk.

Jno. Menzies, Spittalton Farm, by Blair Drummond, Stirling.

Peter Comrie Menzies, Provision and Wine Merchant, Stirling.

Robert Menzies, late Proprietor, Royal George Hotel, Perth.

Robert Menzies, Provision Merchant, Stirling.

Rev. Robert William Menzies, St. James, Clerkenwell, London.

Stuart Menzies, C.A., 55 Hertford Road, Bootle, Liverpool, and 5 Kelvinside Terrace, West, Glasgow.

T. Paton Menzies, C.A., 17 Corleig Road, W., Hampstead London, N.W., and 5 Kelvinside Terrace, West, Glasgow.

Thomas Menzies, Farmer, Spittalton, by Blair Drummond, Stirling.

William Menzies, Builder and Joiner, 37 Kelvinside Street, Glasgow.

Captain William Menzies, 23 Sussex Street, Glasgow.

William C. Menzies, Master of Works, 33 Kelvingrove Street, West, Glasgow.

William Menzies, 12 Society Street, Camlachie, Glasgow.

William John Menzies, Dentist, c o H. C. M'Nair, Georgian Buildings, Portland Oregon, U.S. America.

Mrs. George Menzies, 2 Woodburn Place, Canaan Lane, Edinburgh.

23

Associate and Honorary Members subscribing 2 6. annually.

George Menzies Bruce, 125 North John Street, Glasgow.

Members who subscribe 2 6. annually to the Menzies Clan Society.

A. Russell Menzies, Engineer, c/o Mrs. Boyd, 34 Devon Street, S.S., Glasgow.
Allan Rattray Menzies, Draughtsman, 34 Grove Street, Newcastle-on-Tyne.
Alexander Menzies, 42 Dunard Street, Glasgow.
Alexander Menzies, 113 High Street, Perth.
Alexander Menzies, Upper Borland Park, Auchterarder.
Alexander Menzies, Rosgate, Tullipourie, Perthshire.
Archibald Menzies, Beswallie, Forfar.
Archibald Menzies, 6 Green Lodge Terrace, Greenhead, Glasgow.
Colin Menzies, Engineer, 13 Maxwell Street, Partick, Glasgow.
Charles Stewart Menzies, Glencairn Cottage, Saltcoats.
D. F. Menzies, Commission Agent, 101 St. Vincent Street, Glasgow.
D. W. Menzies, 154 Hope Street, Glasgow.
Daniel W. Menzies, 51 Pollok Street, Glasgow.
David S. Menzies, 13 Maxwell Street, Partick, Glasgow.
Duncan Menzies, Restaurant and Tea Rooms, 14 Mill Street, Perth.
Duncan Menzies, 6 Cambridge Street, Glasgow.
Duncan Menzies, Farmer, Balmacaan, near Ballinluig.
Duncan Menzies, Dundurn Mill, St. Fillans, by Crieff.
Duncan Menzies, 19 Nicol Street, Kirkcaldy.
Duncan Menzies, Joiner, Crachan, by Weem, Aberfeldy.
Finlay Stewart Menzies, Glenlyon Cottage, Pitlochry.
George Menzies, 4 North Park Terrace, Dundee.
Gilbert Menzies, Coachman, Dull, Aberfeldy.
James Menzies, Clan Menzies' Piper, Shenvail, by Weem, Aberfeldy
James Anderson Menzies, c/o Mrs. Murdoch, 64 Merchant Street, Crosshill, Glasgow.
James Menzies, 184 Church Street, Maryhill, Glasgow.
James Menzies, Crachan, by Weem, Aberfeldy.
James Menzies, Puninnee Gardens, by Larbert.
James Menzies, The Rhyddings, Oswald Twistle, Lancashire.
James Rae Menzies, 353 Allison Street, Glasgow.
James Menzies, 27 Crichton Street, Dundee.

Captain James Menzies, 5 Argyle Street, Rothesay.
James Richard Menzies, 5 Weymouth Terrace, Ibrox, Glasgow.
John Menzies, 202 Baltic Street, Bridgeton, Glasgow.
John B. Mennie, 49 Kenilworth Road, Newcastle-on-Tyne.
John Menzies, 129 Shields Road, Glasgow.
John Menzies, Coshieville, by Weem, Aberfeldy.
John Menzies, Edramuir, by Ballinluig.
John Menzies, 41 East London Street, Edinburgh.
John Menzies, Back Dykes, Strathmiglo, Fifeshire.
John Menzies, Logierait Mills, by Ballinluig.
John Stewart Menzies, Reswallie, Forfar.
Malcolm Menzies, 37 Wallacegrove Place, Shields Road, Glasgow.
Peter A. Menzies, 22 Janefield Place, Maryhill, and c/o Watson, 35 Gordon
    Street, Glasgow.
Robert Menzies, 11 Horsell Road, Highbury, N. : or, Head Office, Bank
    of Scotland, London.
Robert Menzies, Farmer, Carse, by Weem, Aberfeldy.
Robert Menzies, Farmer, Tullichville, by Weem, Aberfeldy.
Thomas Menzies, Inspector, 2 Black Street, Glasgow.
Walter Menzies, 7 Janefield Place, Maryhill, Glasgow.
William B. Menzies, Highland Railway Co. Station Master, Strameferry, Ross.
William Menzies, Burn Craig Cottage, Moffat.
Wilfred Roxburgh Menzies, 22 Holmwood Road, Liverpool.
William Brownlee Menzies, Burnside Terrace, Camelon, Falkirk.
William Menzies, 205 Wolseley Street, Glasgow.
William Menzies, Weem, by Aberfeldy.
William Menzies, Tychraggan, Weem, Aberfeldy.
William Menzies, Logierait Mill, by Ballinluig.
William Menzies, Reswallie, Forfar.
William Menzies, Provision Merchant, 34 Dunkeld Street, Aberfeldy.
William Menzies, Store Keeper, 94 Church Street, Inverness.
Miss Caroline Menzies, Glenmore, Princess Park, Liverpool.
Mrs. Menzies, Lady of the late Surgeon-General Duncan Menzies.
Miss Emily Menzies, daughter of the late Surgeon-General Duncan
    Menzies, 23 Westbourne Park Road, Bayswater, London, W.
Miss Isobel Menzies, Brown Street, Bridgeton.
Mrs. Ada Menzies, Derby Street, Andover, Massachusetts, U.S. America.
Miss R. Menzies, daughter of Rev. J. H. Menzies, 54 Grove Street, New-
    castle-on-Tyne.
Miss Susan Menzies, 7 Royal Terrace, West Kingston, Co. Dublin.
Miss Kate Menzies, 7 Royal Terrace, West Kingston, Co. Dublin.
Miss M. Jessie Menzies, 7 Royal Terrace, West Kingston, Co. Dublin.

25

DONATIONS to the Collection of Reliques, etc., etc., presented to the Menzies Clan Society.

First Donation presented to the Menzies Clan Society, by Thomas Menzies, Esq., 22 Marchmount Road, Edinburgh.

No. 1.—A Silver Flask made out of the First Prize Medals, won by Thomas Menzies, the great Athlete, the father of the donor. These Medals were gained at the principal Highland and Athletic Games in England and Scotland, between the years 1839 and 1854. He was also the winner of the Gold Champion Medal for Scotland, at Leith, in 1844, and at London in 1851, he was successful in defeating all opponents, and was declared Champion of Great Britain, for which he was awarded the Gold Champion Medal.

Second Donation by Robert Menzies, Esq., J.P., Tirinie, near Aberfeldy.

No. 2-3.—The Powder Horn and Water Flask of Ian Menzies, of Shian and Glenquiech, who was Colonel of the Menzies Regiment, who were formed by him in support of the House of Stuart in 1745-46, and who fought for Bonnie Prince Charlie through the whole of the Rebellion, and greatly distinguished himself at Prestonpans, Clifton, Falkirk, and specially at Culloden. His son is the hero of the "Vich Ian Vor" of Sir Walter Scott's Waverley. The donor, Robert Menzies, Tirinie, is a descendant of his.

Third, by D. P. Menzies, F.S.A., Scot., 4 Holyrood Quadrant, Glasgow.

No. 4.—Book of Poems, by George Menzies the poet, born in 1797 in Kincardineshire, where he was brought up, being one of the offshoots of the Menzies' of Pitfodels. He went out to Canada when about 37 years of age, and at first became assistant school master at the Academy at Niagra, afterwards he became the editor of the "Niagra Reporter," then of the "St. Catherine's Journal," and in 1840 he commenced as proprietor the newspaper named "Woodstock" in the district of Brock, now the county of Oxford, where he was fairly successful. He was highly esteemed all over Western Canada, as a man, a poet, and a politician, died 25th February, 1847.

No. 5.—Book by Sutherland Menzies, "History of the Middle Ages." He is also the author of many other works.

No. 6.—Book by Louisa Menzies, "Lives of the Greek Heroines." She is also the author of other works.

26

Fourth Donation presented by Lieut. Colonel Duncan Menzies, Bars h, Rogart, Sutherlandshire.

No. 7.—Gaelic Poems by Archibald Menzies, "Orian Gaidhelach." He. when a young man went to Australia. One of his poems evidently refers to his voyage, &c. Having made some money there, on his return he had the Dreadnought Hotel at Callander for several years, and died at Edinburgh.

No. 8.—"The History of France," by Sutherland Menzies. Presented by by Rector Thomas Menzies, J.P., F.E.I.S., Hutcheson's Grammar Schools, Crown Street, Glasgow.

No. 9.—"America as a Field for Investment," by William John Menzies, Esq., W.S. Presented to the Society by the Author. Published with Map, by William Blackwood & Sons, Edinburgh and London.

No. 10.—"The Drainage of Glasgow and the Pollution of the Clyde," by William Menzies, Deputy-Surveyor of Windsor Parks and Forests to her Majesty the Queen. Presented by his son, William Menzies, Esq., Englefield Green, Surrey.

OBITUARY AND BIOGRAPHY.

It is with deep regret that we have to record the death of our Clansman—
ALEXANDER MENZIES, farmer, Tegarnach, Dull. He was one of the keenest and most successful farmers on the estates of the Chief, Sir R. bert Menzies, Baronet of Menzies. He received a sore in which led to the amputation of his leg from the effects of which he never recovered. He was an enthusiastic Volunteer in the 30th battalion of the Black Watch, and was much esteemed by all who had the pleasure of knowing him. For about 20 years he served under the Colonelship of the "The Chief," and was Sergeant of the Aberfeldy Company. He was a good rifle shot, one year taking first prize in his company. He also won a number of trophies and medals in local competitions, and at the Edinburgh annual meeting gained the Bronze Medal. He died at Dull, 29th August, 1894, aged about 57.

With the deepest sorrow we have also to record the death of our esteemed Clanswoman—
Mrs. JOHN MENZIES, daughter of Major Archibald Menzies of the 42nd Highlanders, celebrated for his deeds at Quatre Bras. She was

born at Farleyer, near Weem, 10th July, 1803, and married John
Menzies, proprietor of the Weem Hotel, where her kindly disposition
made her much beloved in the country round and throughout the
Appin na Menearich. On her family becoming ripe for the University, they removed to Edinburgh where she had the satisfaction of seeing
her sons become men of note and distinction : (1) Robert becoming
a Colonel V.D.J.P. and S.S.C.—(2) James also becoming a Colonel,
V.D.—(3) Archibald, a Major, V.A.S.S.C.—Thomas also being a
successful business man in New Zealand. She passed away on the
27th October, 1894, at the venerable age of 93, and was laid to rest
in the parish kirkyard of Dull in the *Appin Na Menearich*.

RONALD STEWART MENZIES (Bolfracks), the younger son of Major James
Stewart Menzies, 93 Victoria Place, Perth. He was born in Perth
and was a young and promising Clansmen, and was trained a banker.
Being in the service of the bank of India at Bombay, from which he
received a higher appointment to their Calcutta office, where he had
only been a few days, when he was suddenly seized by a malady,
and died at the age of 29 years of age, at Calcutta, 22nd February,
1895, and was buried the same day in the Scottish Cemetry there.

Major JAMES STEWART MENZIES late 74th Highlanders, 73 Victoria Place,
Perth. He was one of the direct descendants of the Menzies Chieftains of Bolfracks, a cousin of the last Baron who held the territory of
Bolfracks. He possessed the Menzies of Bolfracks Claymore. He
served with the 74th Highlanders in India, where he greatly distinguished himself at the storming of Fort Kopal, there he at the
head of a detachment of Highlanders drove the enemy from their
fortifications ; for this campaign he received a medal. He was the
father of the above, and being aged, he never recovered the sudden
news of his son's death, and died at the grand old age of 82 years on
14th August, 1895. To the last he had the distinguishing mien of a
soldier and a Menzies.

Deputy Superintendant JOHN MENZIES, 11 Eglinton Terrace, Ayr. He was a
splendid specimen of a Menzies, being over 6 feet in height. In his
younger days he was in the army, being sergeant-major in the
transport corps served his country through the Crimean War, &c.
On returning from the army he became deputy-superintendant of the
Ayr Police, where he was much respected and esteemed. He was
born in the village of Strathmiglo, Fifeshire, and died at the age of
64, on the 5th March, 1895.

Dr. JOHN DUNCAN MENZIES, M.B., Royal Navy, was one of the most distinguished Naval Surgeons of his time. He entered the service 28th

February, 1887, and was appointed to the flagship Duke of Wellington. Thereafter he served on board the Impregnable and the Magpie. It was during the expedition to the West Coast of Africa in 1890-91 on board the Magpie that his self-sacrificing and gallant services won for him the award of the "Gilbert Blane Bronze Medal," a distinction that very few in the British Navy have. he was the youngest surgeon who had it conferred on him. He also served on H.M.S. Suspered, Sharpshooter, Steelwell, and Falcon, from which, being ill, he was taken to the R.N. Hospital, Portland, where he died at the early age of 34, beloved by all the British Tars who have had the gentle, kind, and skilled hand of Dr. Menzies to relieve their pain. He was a descendant of the Menzies' of Comrie.

He was the son of Surgeon-General Duncan Menzies, who so ably commanded the Medical Staff during the Crimean War, having the Hospitals at Scutari under his charge. He was born in Dull, in the *Appin na Menarich* in the Menzies estates, Perthshire, and was traditionally descended from the Menzies' of Comrie.

CHARLES MENZIES, Esq., 136 Victoria Road, Glasgow, builder and property proprietor, born about 1850. He was one of the most enthusiastic members of the Menzies Clan Society, being a well known figure at all the gatherings and meetings of the Society where he always appeared in "The Kilt" of Menzies hunting tartan. His vigorous and spirited style made him a favourite with his clansmen. He was the father of thirteen children, and was quite active until a few days before his death which took place on the 25th December, 1895. He was a descendant of the Menzies of Culter.

JOHN MENZIES, Esq., of the Banavie Hotel, was a native of the *Appin na Menarich*, being born 7th June, 1830, on the Menzies estates, and in early life was educated for the learned professions, but circumstances prevented the carrying out of this intention. In turning his energies to business he chose Highland hotel-keeping, at Birnam, Inverness, and Banavie. In this he had the art of making visitors to his hotel "at Home." His kindly, cheery, and hearty welcome, with his obliging disposition made a stay at his hotel a real pleasure. He died 15th October, 1895, at Banavie, and was laid to rest in Warriston Cemetery, Edinburgh. He was 66 years of age. Advocate A. J. P. Menzies, M.A., author of several works on Law is his son and only child.

TELEGRAPHIC ADDRESS—"SILVERSMITH, GLASGOW"
TELEPHONE NO. 3475.

Thomas Smith & Son,

...Manufacturing Silversmiths,...

31 QUEEN STREET, GLASGOW.

Makers of Articles in
Solid Silver for Presentation,
&c. and Highest Class Electro-Plate
for General Use.

Menzies'
Crest . .
Brooch.

Silver, . 10 6

Electro-
Plate, . 3 .

Crest Buttons.

Silver, · - 2 6 each.

Electro-Plate. 1 3 ,,

THE BATH HOTEL,

152 BATH STREET, GLASGOW.

The Most Comfortable First-Class Hotel in Glasgow.

NEWLY RE-DECORATED.

BEDROOM, WITH ATTENDANCE FROM 2s 6d

CHARGES STRICTLY MODERATE.

Purveyor for Clan Meetings, Dinners, &c., &c.

Telephone No. 229.　　　　P. Robertson, Proprietor.